About the Book

Take a compact motor and some pedals, blend them nicely together on a heavy-duty bicycle frame, and you have a mo-ped. After gaining wide favor in Europe, these mighty little two-stroke engine machines are now making a far-reaching mark in this country. Because mo-peds get terrific mileage and are easy to maintain, they are perfect machines for taking you to school, for getting you to work, and for making light shopping trips. They are also great for just plain fooling around. Author Jerry Murray takes a good look at the strong and weak points of the different brands and tells you what each machine requires to keep it running, and running, and running.

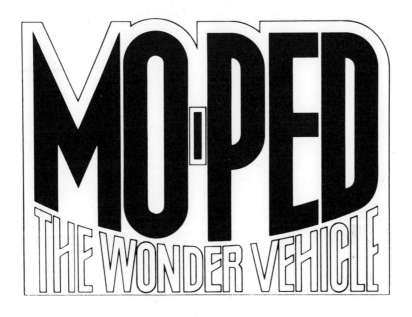

MO·PED
THE WONDER VEHICLE

JERRY MURRAY

G. P. PUTNAM'S SONS, NEW YORK

*Photos courtesy of the author except as follows:
pp. 59 and 65 courtesy Batavus; pp. 11 and 113
courtesy Bombardier-Puch; p. 89 courtesy Cimatti;
p. 91 courtesy Gitane; p. 85 courtesy Kreidler;
pp. 97 and 101 courtesy Solo Electric.*

Library of Congress Cataloging in Publication Data
Murray, Jerry
Mo-Ped, The Wonder Vehicle. Includes index.
Summary: Describes an individual motorized form of
transportation successfully used in Europe, its
advantages, maintenance, and distinctive brands.
1. Mopeds-Juvenile literature. [1. Mopeds]
I. Title.
TL443.M8   629.22'72   76-18937

PRINTED IN THE UNITED STATES OF AMERICA
10 up

Contents

MO-PED
The Wonder Vehicle

1 What Is a Mo-Ped?

Take a compact motor and some pedals, blend them together on a heavy-duty bicycle frame, and you have a mo-ped.

It has been done countless times by tinkerers, but it took European designers to come up with a mass produced mo-ped that works consistently. It's what *Popular Mechanics* magazine described as "the cheapest and most economical form of individual motorized transportation known to Europe." The mo-ped, a little machine that Europe exploited a number of years ago, has great possibilities in present-day, energy-conscious America.

Remembering that the word comes from *mo*tor and *ped*al, it's something for Americans to hold in mind these days. Mo-peds are made for taking you to school, to go shopping, or for just fooling around. They are so sturdy and reliable, they have crossed the Sahara Desert on camel trails, carried loads three times their own weight, and at least one crossed the country from the Atlantic to the Pacific, averaging 157 miles per gallon.

That average means less than an ounce of fuel was used for every full mile. It's extraordinary mileage, when you realize that the average American passenger car consumes over an ounce of gasoline in just firing up and getting its driver out of the gas station.

A mo-ped is also easy to maintain. You don't have to worry about taking it into the garage for an oil change or any expensive mechanical adjustments. If you're not afraid to do it yourself, routine maintenance can be done in half an hour for half a dollar. The young man who rode his mo-ped from Florida to California spent a total of about one hour doing his maintenance along the way. He removed, cleaned, and replaced his spark plug four times en route, and he took his carburetor apart and cleaned its jet once. He did these chores without the aid of a factory-trained mechanic, and he used nothing but the tools that came with his mo-ped in its handy tool kit.

Most of all, a mo-ped is fun to ride. It's a joy to tromp down the nearest pedal and hear its motor start to purr. No electric starter, driven by a thirty-dollar battery. No automatic choke that you're not quite sure is operating. It's not a car, it's a mo-ped, and its starter is your foot. But it's not a motorcycle, either. If something is a bit sour in the motor—and this can always happen when you have a mechanical device—you don't have to kick and kick to start. Just climb on and pedal down the road—give it a little exercise to clear out its one lung—and, *poof!* the cold motor catches hold, and you're off to enjoy the real pleasure of mo-ped riding.

You have to go slowly. The mo-ped will only do twenty-

The handsome, sturdy Puch typifies today's mo-ped—49 cc motor,
25 to 30 mph, no gear shifting, and well over 100 miles per gallon.

five or thirty miles per hour. On busy streets you have to stay over to the right much of the time. This lets cars pass you so that they can wait for you at the next stop signal. Mo-ped riding on country roads makes up for busy highways, however, since your leisurely pace does not frighten away wild life.

The mo-ped does not take the place of the car or the motorcycle. It is definitely slower. It cannot comfortably carry a passenger for any distance. But it does have its importance in our American way of life. That importance grows daily as our fuel resources shrink. The mo-ped's function is to provide you with simple, economical, entertaining transportation that gives you the freedom to get around on your own.

2 Learning to Live with Your Mo-Ped

There are quite a few different brands of mo-peds available throughout the world, but only a limited number for sale here in America. To be a true mo-ped, as opposed to a motorcycle with pedals, all these different machines have five things in common:

All have bicycle pedals.

All have two wheels.

All have an engine, almost always gasoline-powered and two-stroke, always with a displacement of less than fifty cubic centimeters (cc).

All have a maximum speed of thirty miles per hour.

All have an automatic clutch or transmission and need no gear-shifting.

Let's look at the pedals first. There are several reasons for having pedals on a mo-ped. Most important, pedals get the motor started. Remember at all times that your mo-ped is a very basic, economical vehicle. No electric starters here because electric starters cost money and electric starters break down, and breakdowns cost still more money. Good advice when you're shopping for a vehicle is to remember Murphy's Law, which says that if anything can go wrong, it will. Mo-ped designers, aware of this possibility, put pedals on their machines instead of electric starters. Some mo-peds can only be fired up as they're being pedaled down the street, but most mo-peds can be started at rest, on their kickstands.

Second, the pedals are your low gear. By any standards at all, the mo-ped is a low-powered machine. It's built to carry you along on level ground at twenty-five or thirty miles an hour. But it slows down carrying you up a hill. If the hill is steep, the clutch begins to slip and smoke and even burn up, unless you help it with your legs. At about ten miles an hour you stop using the pedals as footrests and help out the machine. The same applies if you want a quicker start from a stop signal. Your feet can help your machine accelerate to five or ten miles an hour when the engine can take you on up to cruising speed. You don't have to use the pedals at all to get yourself off from a stop, but it extends the life of your engine and clutch.

And the pedals are there if you run out of gas. This can happen. When you're getting a hundred and fifty miles to the gallon, you forget to make frequent stops for gas and oil. There is not a mo-ped made with a gas gauge; most have fuel cocks. One position is for shutting off the fuel flow when parked, a second is for cruising with a full tank, and a third is for tapping a small reserve supply to get you home or to a gas station when you run out. Some mo-peds, however, don't have the fuel cock. They are such simplified machines that you must look inside the gas tank to check your supply. Most mo-peds have a button or lever that will disengage the engine from the wheel and make pedaling easier, but even those without this handy feature can be pedaled. Don't expect any of them to pedal like your old ten-speed. The best pedaling mo-peds might be compared to a stingray-type bicycle. They have short pedal cranks, so it takes a lot of turns of the feet to get up a decent speed and sustain it. And the mo-ped is, of course, heavier than a bicycle. Nevertheless, those pedals can be a great help at times.

Suppose, for example, you want to go to school on your mo-ped, and the school authorities don't allow motor vehicles on campus. Just motor to school, then kill the motor and pedal on to the bike rack.

There are three-wheeled mo-peds, used almost entirely as delivery vehicles, but it takes a rider with a good deal of balance to be able to handle one, especially with a load. You can plan to ride a two-wheeled mo-ped. It is a very safe machine. According to European statistics, it is about fourteen percent safer than a bicycle. Its tires are fatter than bicycle tires and provide better traction in turns. And the rider is sitting upright, not bent over turned-down handlebars where he can't see around him as well as he should. One of the biggest safety features in comparison with a bicycle is that the bike goes much faster and takes much longer to stop. Sixty miles an hour isn't too great a problem for the diligent ten-speed pedaler; but it does become a problem when he must make an emergency stop with nothing but caliper brakes and two inches of rubber on the road. Mo-peds usually are equipped with expanding drum brakes.

There are forty-nine cubic centimeters of displacement in a mo-ped's engine because of the laws in most countries oriented to the vehicle. These laws sensibly state that any two-wheeler with a displacement of less than fifty cubic centimeters is not a motorcycle and thus may be driven without the need for a standard driver's license.

This means a great deal in some countries. In Switzerland, for instance, it is not uncommon to pay a thousand dollars for driving instruction that might last for six months before you are even qualified to take the very rigorous driver's test. In Germany the sales tax is waived when you buy a two-wheeler of less than fifty cubic centimeters displacement. The German and the Swiss laws and others in other countries discourage the use of big gas-guzzling automobiles and encourage the use of the economical and safe small machine. They are not arbitrary laws by any means, and they were worked out over the years in close cooperation with cycle manufacturers.

Through trial and error it was found that one can travel around safely and easily on a motor of forty-nine cubic centimeters. It's so easy to operate that in most European countries you can legally ride one on the streets when you're only ten years old.

Here in America, state by state, we are following suit in similar recognition of the mo-ped, and the driver's requirements are easing off. It has been a long time in coming. Legislators were concerned about losing revenue unless a mo-ped has a license. They worried about safety factors. Many simply didn't know what a mo-ped was. But work and education are improving the future of the mo-ped in this country.

At least one United States firm tried to build a modern mo-ped here to take advantage of the gasoline crisis, but failed. It couldn't compete with the years of experience European mo-ped makers have behind them.

The American manufacturer failed because he never really got to know what he was trying to build. On the other hand, European and Asian builders of mo-peds ride them constantly and seek ways to improve them. These people traditionally are more frugal than Americans, though just as fun-loving, so they find it no chore to ride to work on a mo-ped instead of in a big gas-wasting auto. They enjoy the freedom of the road just as much as we do, but they enjoy that freedom just as happily on a hundred-pound machine as one can in a two-ton car. So we'll look to the Europeans for our mo-ped experience and technology.

A mo-ped's spoked wheels may be driven by a friction roller, a rubber vee belt, a steel chain, or some combination of these. But the driving force behind any is that forty-nine cubic centimeter engine. And that engine is always a two-stroke engine.*

The displacement of the engine is simply the usable volume of the combustion chamber. It is the area of the piston multiplied by the distance the piston travels in centimeters. Everything about the mo-ped is in the metric system.

Some of these metric measurements are converted to the United States system for your easy reference, but others stand as they are and will help you get acquainted with the

---

* Honda made a four-stroke mo-ped of forty-nine cubic centimeters, the P-50. A few of them arrived in this country before their place in the cargo ships was taken over by the 350, the 750, then the Honda 1000 motorcycles.

metric system, which will be our standard here eventually. The engine displacement then comes out in cubic centimeters instead of cubic inches, and it is a two-stroke engine because two-stroke is better than four-stroke for a machine of this size. It's simpler. It delivers more power for its size. The four-stroke engine has camshafts and poppet valves and an oil-filled crankcase with an oil pump. The two-stroke eliminates all of these. The two-stroke still has a crankcase, a crankshaft, and a piston; it has breaker points and condenser, but a great many complexities of the automotive-type engine aren't needed in the two-stroke motorcycle and mo-ped engine. It is simple and compact, but you do pay a price for this.

In a car gallons of gasoline go in a tank at the back and quarts of oil go into a sump under the engine. Not so with the two-stroke engine. Gasoline and oil go into the same tank, with the oil doing its lubricating job as it proceeds with the gasoline to the combustion chamber, where most of it is burned up with the power-producing gasoline. On a big, sophisticated two-stroke motorcycle or motor scooter, the oil goes into a separate tank to be automatically mixed with the gasoline in the carburetor. But on the simple mo-ped, where your legs are called on to help make it move, your hands are called on to premix the oil with the gasoline.

It isn't such a big chore. Some people do it at home in a gas can, others do it at the gas station. Any decent mo-ped comes with some sort of a measuring cup for the oil and has instructions about just how much oil to use for the amount of gasoline your tank needs. You'll usually carry enough oil in a small plastic bottle to take care of one tankful of gasoline,

A mo-ped's power plant. Ten pounds or so of two-stroke motor are all that is really needed to get you around town or across country.

then refill the oil bottle next time you're home. The mixing is a little messy at first, but it soon becomes routine. Since you'll get more than a hundred miles per gallon of gas, it doesn't have to be done very often. But it definitely does have to be done each time you fuel up your machine.

Ordinary motor oil may be used in a pinch, but specially compounded two-stroke oil is recommended. This contains additives to help it burn more completely in your combustion chamber, and it has all the lubricating qualities that the two-stroke engine needs. Use good two-stroke oil. Use the best. Mix oil and gasoline yourself, so you're certain it's done correctly.

The oil and gas mix flows to the carburetor where it's mixed with air. From there it goes to the crankcase, and finally to the combustion chamber. It is sucked in by the movement of the piston, compressed by that piston, and ignited by the spark plug to make your machine move. A lot of things are happening in the crankcase and combustion chamber. In very rapid succession, sometimes in overlapping sequence, fuel is being sucked in, compressed, ignited, and the burned gases are being pushed out through the exhaust port and muffler.

In an automobile engine these things are happening, too, but in that kind of engine the piston moves up and down two times for each time the spark plug fires once. In the two-stroke engine, that plug fires every time the piston reaches the top of its thrust. The two-stroke engine, then, is theoretically twice as busy as the four-stroke and theoretically produces twice as much power per engine revolution. The first price you pay for this increased efficiency is in having to mix your own gasoline and oil. The second price you pay is in the process fondly known as de-coking.

De-coking is simply the removal of carbon buildup from the combustion chamber. No matter how good your oil is, it won't burn completely with the gasoline. If it did, it would not have the lubricating properties to keep your mo-ped buzzing. Some of the oil is burned, some is exhausted unburned through the muffler, and some gets only partially burned and ends up as carbon or coke. This deposits on the piston, inside the cylinder head, in the exhaust port, and in the muffler.

As these deposits slowly accumulate, they reduce the size of the combustion chamber and constrict the exhaust port to a point where your engine can't breathe properly. When the combustion chamber is reduced in size, the engine can't get a full charge of air and gasoline. When the exhaust port size is reduced, the burned gases can't get completely expelled.

All this shows up gradually in sluggish performance. After four or five thousand miles, you find your mo-ped doing only twenty-one or twenty-two miles per hour instead of its original twenty-five, and you find yourself working the pedals halfway up a hill instead of near the top. It feels as if your machine is simply wearing out, and there's a temptation at this point to sell the weary old thing or trade it in on a new one. Don't do it. Get out your metric wrenches instead and settle down to an hour or two of dirty work. De-coke your mo-ped when it needs it, and it will run like new again.

But only de-coke when it's called for. Just because your mo-ped is performing sluggishly, don't tear the motor down. It could be that the timing is a little off or the breaker

21

De-coking means pulling this head and cylinder and muffler, and carefully scraping off the accumulated carbon deposits. Using the best two-stroke oil can delay the de-coking chore for a long time.

points are dirty or simply that the spark plug is shot. The quickest, most positive way to find out if your mo-ped's two-stroke engine needs de-coking is to remove the muffler and look for a coke buildup just inside the muffler's intake. Scrape through the carbon with a pick. If there's more than two or three millimeters (about one sixteenth of an inch) of caked carbon there, your machine could stand a de-coking.

First remove the cylinder head and the cylinder, and then start scraping. Many mo-peds have a compression release valve in the cylinder head. The name is more formidable than the device itself. Just pay attention to how it's put together on the cylinder head when you remove it, and put it back together in the same way. Scrape carefully, because you don't want to damage the metal surfaces. Remove the coke as completely as you can, but don't let the scrapings fall back inside the crankcase because they'll damage the bearings there. Take your time, do it right, and you won't have to do it again for more thousands of miles.

Disassemble the compression release mechanism from the cylinder head and clean it, making sure it operates smoothly. You might use a dab of valve grinding compound to reface the valve seat here. Work slowly and thoughtfully, remembering at all times that you've got to put the whole works back together again when that carbon has been removed. Get a coffee can or a jar to put the nuts and bolts and washer in as you remove them.

With care, you can reuse the cylinder gasket, but it's a better idea to get a new one from your mo-ped dealer before you tackle the de-coking. Sometimes the best idea is to let him do the whole job. Trust your dealer to do it right, but take off that muffler and inspect it before you take your mo-ped to him, just to be certain your machine really does need it.

Be especially careful in scraping the coke from the piston. The piston and its head are aluminum, and therefore soft. Remove all the carbon from the ports in the piston—which are the holes in its sides. While you're at it, make sure the piston rings are working freely. If they are not, replace them.

Naturally, the less oil you use, the longer you can postpone de-coking. Three percent of oil instead of the recommended four should build up only three quarters as much coke. Don't be tempted—like the farmer who was training his plow horse to get along on a smaller amount of expensive oats and hay. Each day the farmer reduced his horse's feed by half. He finally reached a point where he wasn't feeding his horse anything at all, but on the day he reached this point the horse died.

If you don't use enough oil, if you use less than the manufacturer recommended, your engine will choke up and die. The piston will seize. If you cruise on straight gasoline, your engine will get hotter until your aluminum piston suddenly melts around the steel piston rings and fuses itself to the iron cylinder wall. That makes the engine stop quickly, and it becomes very difficult to start again. The pedals come in handy when you have a piston seizure, too, but follow the mixing instructions and use a good grade of oil, and there is no reason in the world for you ever to have a piston seizure.

If you use too much oil, of course, you'll have to de-coke

prematurely. And you'll be forever fouling your spark plug. Use a good quality two-stroke oil, and use it in the right amount.

Your mo-ped has one cylinder and two spark plugs. One of the plugs is screwed into your cylinder head, popping away with the steady beat that keeps the mo-ped going. It is also accumulating carbon deposits of its own, and it is slowly but continually changing its gap setting. A magneto squirts high voltage, low amperage electricity to the spark plug to shoot a hot blue spark across the plug's electrodes and fire the gas/oil/air mixture. The gap between those electrodes is important since the magneto can only deliver just so much electricity to the hard-working plug. If the gap is too narrow, the spark will be a measly one, sometimes not enough to get good performance at high speeds. If the gap is too wide, the spark won't make it at low speeds and your mo-ped will be hard to start and hard to keep idling.

Keep the gap close to the recommended setting. Each time that spark plug fires, a few molecules of metal are ripped off from your electrode. When you figure your spark plug is firing something like four thousand times each minute, you can see how it adds up. Thus, after four or five hundred miles of running, take out your spark plug, clean it, reset the gap, and screw it back in the cylinder head. Your mo-ped will come with a spark plug wrench in its tool kit, just for this purpose. And in that tool kit should be your second spark plug.

If a spark plug fouls on you while you're on the road, dismount and change it. Even a brand new plug can foul out. It takes only a small particle of carbon to lodge between the electrodes and completely eliminate your sparking ability. You can remove the plug and clean it at this point, but you're probably in a hurry and the spark plug is hot, so carry an extra one for a quick change and be on your way. Put the old, fouled plug in your tool kit and clean and regap it when you get home.

Always use the right plug. Every spark plug has its own heat range; each operates best at a certain temperature. If you're running a plug that's too hot for your machine you'll get excellent performance—until it burns a hole in your piston. If your plug is too cold for your engine, your machine will run more like a bicycle than a mo-ped.

A mo-ped has a maximum speed of thirty miles an hour strictly for safety reasons. With a lot of engine tinkering and a lot of gearing, one mo-ped was made to go in excess of a hundred and twenty miles an hour. It was not, however, very safe, and so your mo-ped will have one, maybe two gears, and a top speed of a sane and sensible thirty miles an hour. This is something else that all modern mo-peds have in common.

The modern mo-ped has as a common feature an automatic clutch or transmission. There is no shifting of gears on a mo-ped. Again this is for safety reasons, for ease of operation. The automatic feature is accomplished with a centrifugal mechanism. That is, as the clutch or the transmission reaches a certain speed, weights swing outward on springs to engage the driving mechanism. No manual clutch on a mo-ped, no kick shifting—just get on it and ride.

And the last thing all mo-peds have in common with each

other is the owner's manual. There's a lot in it. Read it. As soon as you get your mo-ped, before you ride it any distance at all, sit down with your owner's manual and read it from cover to cover. Keep it in a safe place. Use it for future reference while you fully enjoy the pleasures and the freedom your mo-ped gives you.

3 Beginnings

A device known as the Whizzer was the grandfather of the American mo-ped. It came in kit form, and if you followed the directions diligently, you could wind up by converting your bicycle into a pretty good mo-ped. Whizzers carried more than a few young Americans along at a giddy twenty miles per hour until they were replaced by automobiles and later by the ubiquitous Japanese motorcycle.

The Whizzer was a simple enough device, a small motor mounted directly behind the saddle, driving the rear wheel by means of a belt. The fact that it spluttered and faltered and failed fairly often was more than made up for by the prestige it gave its owner.

The young person with the Whizzer towered head and shoulders over his friends with mere bicycles. He had all the mobility they had plus stamina that was limited only by his gasoline budget. In the days when gasoline cost only twenty cents a gallon, one could buy a lot of stamina. Anyone who owned a Whizzer felt it could do everything but leap tall buildings in a single bound.

There were several other early American mo-peds. The Singer Company made a three-wheeler as well as a two-wheeler before settling down to manufacturing sewing machines. The Indian Company made more than 100,000 mo-peds before diverting to other things and then going out of business. The Thor was a good mo-ped. The Peerless did well, and the Flying Merkel is still remembered as a good machine.

Away back in 1884 the Copeland Company made a steam-driven mo-ped on a high-wheeler frame. Various manufacturers placed the motor at various locations—on the front wheel, the back wheel, between the wheels, and even behind them. Others offered conversion kits for changing your bicycle into a mo-ped as the Whizzer company did. The mo-ped was very popular in this country early in the twentieth century, but people were lured to faster, bigger machines. The Model-T Ford was one of the machines that drove the Whizzer out of existence.

The mo-ped turned into a novelty item in this country, but in Europe it caught on and endured. Gasoline prices were always high in Europe, cars were considered more of a luxury than a necessity there, and highway planners did their work with small vehicles in mind as well as cars and trucks and buses. In Europe children watched with envy as their father left for work. It was almost as popular with women as men. If the family was lucky enough to own a car, it was largely reserved for family outings, while the bicycle and the mo-ped were relied on for the daily shopping and commuting. More than a dozen brands of early mo-peds enjoyed immediate success in Europe. Some evolved into motorcycles, others were greatly improved upon. But one has survived almost intact to exist as the living, working grand-daddy of the large family of mo-peds in the world today.

It is called the Solex, and it has been manufactured at the Paris factory of the Velosolex Company for over thirty years. *Cycle World* magazine called the Solex 3800 "the slowest, cheapest, blackest, front-wheel drive two-wheeler in the history of mankind." *Cycle World* was accurate in this description. The Solex that the magazine road-tested several years ago could then be purchased for about a hundred and fifty dollars in Europe.

The recently introduced American model, the 4600, sells for more than twice that price now because of inflation and because of the extra safety equipment decreed by our Federal agencies. Nevertheless, the Solex is about the cheapest mo-ped you can buy and one of the most reliable. The model number, by the way, doesn't signify anything at all.

Velosolex started off with a Model 1700, made some changes a few years later and called it their Model 2200, improved it again and stuck the 3800 label on it. The manufacturer jazzed it up by offering a variety of colors, adding rising handlebars, and changing the motor-actuating lever, and this model was called the 5000. Then the company went back to the number 4600 for the chrome-trimmed, more highly illuminated machine that's coming in quantities to America. With minor exceptions, all these models are basically the same. The 3800 is still made in vast quantities. This is the machine we'll examine closely, for it is the one that retains the true Solex image.

The 3800 is ingeniously simple. A black, heavy-duty

bicycle frame with no springs other than in the seat, it has a ten-pound motor that's mounted on the steering yoke on top of the front wheel. The engine spins a ceramic spool, which in turn rolls against the front tire to pull the little sixty-pounder over the cobblestoned European streets and—with a pedal assist—up the hills.

By reaching over the handlebars and grabbing a lever that sticks up, you can pull the whole works up off the wheel and use the Solex as a straight, one-speed bicycle to coast down a hill or to get some on-the-level exercise. By jamming the engine down on the wheel and closing the compression release valve, you get some more help on the next hill. It's all very compact, and although the bulgy contrivance squatting in front of the handlebars can't be accused of being beautiful, it does give the Solex a no-nonsense appearance of simple mechanical dignity.

There's a 1.5-liter gas tank on the right side of the motor and a balancing, plastic-shrouded magneto-flywheel on the left. The single cylinder of forty-nine cubic centimeters sticks straight up, just to the right of the heavy-spoked front wheel. The crankshaft runs over the top of the wheel through a ceramic spool to a simple and not too efficient centrifugal clutch, and beyond to the mag-flywheel. The clutch is attached back to that ceramic spool that does the job on the wheel. It's simple as can be, and it works.

A four percent gas-oil mix goes in the tank, and the tank comes with its own measuring cup. Just unscrew the gas cap and there it is in your hand. Three gas caps full of thirty-weight motorcycle oil go into each tank of gasoline, and you're ready to roll.

This is the Solex motor, with fuel tank on the left, mag-flywheel on the right, and vertical cylinder turning the friction-drive roller against the front tire.

The carburetors of more sophisticated mo-peds are fed by gravity, but the archaic Solex has a fuel pump. It's a little thing about the size of a book of matches, mounted on the front of the crankcase. There's a rubber diaphragm and a tiny plastic ball inside the fuel pump. In back of the pump a hole leads inside the crankcase. Each time the piston moves, the crankcase pressure changes and activates the diaphragm, sucking fuel mix out of the tank and pushing it up to the carburetor, which is located around the other side of the cylinder. Its only problem is that the fuel pump works too well, pumping far more gas-oil than could ever be used by the little engine. But the carburetor takes care of this little problem in overabundance.

Velosolex makes carburetors for Volkswagens and Porsches—highly sophisticated things with floats and needle valves and multiple jets, carburetors that are far more complex than the whole Solex 3800 put together. Their mo-ped carburetor has no float, no needle valve, and only one tiny jet, but the thing works very well. That little fuel pump delivers torrents of gas-oil to the carburetor, all of which flows past the single jet, which takes what it needs to run, then lets the rest flow right on down a neoprene tube and back into the fuel tank. Who needs a bulky float and needle valve with this sort of arrangement?

The carburetor is operated by the traditional twist grip handgrip on the right-hand side. Twist it away from you and the 3800 will slow down from its giddy twenty miles per hour so you can squeeze that weird, upside-down brake lever. Or just squeeze the lever and the carburetor is automatically shut down as the brakes take their bite. Those clever Frenchmen have run the front brake cable through the carburetor control so that it cuts back on the gas feed as it goes on its way to the caliper front brakes. This charming feature, sad to say, has been eliminated on the new, improved American 4600. C849982 CO. SCHOOLS

There is one clever thing after another on the Solex. As ungainly looking as it is, it's a classic machine of which its inventors should be proud. The company sells so many in other parts of the world that until recently it hasn't made much sales effort in this country. As our highway safety requirements became more stringent, necessitating more lighting requirements on all vehicles, the Solex remained exactly where it was, with one pale yellow headlight and usually no brake light at all.

Several American businessmen have imported shiploads of black Solex 3800s, only to go broke trying either to make them comply with United States laws or trying to change those laws. But with the advent of the 4600, things are changing. The 4600 is festooned with a sealed beam headlight, oversized tail light, front- and rear-brake lights. It comes in pretty reds and blues and yellows and greens, and its handle levers are pointed in the right direction. But underneath all the electric jewelry and paint, it's still the same dawn-age mo-ped.

There is no firing up while resting on the stand with the Solex. You start up by setting the choke, pushing the engine down on the wheel, depressing the compression-release valve, and pedaling away. Within a few meters let go of the compression-release valve and away you go. New or old, the Solex will start up pretty easily.

There are quite a few old Solexes scattered around the country, and since they're so similar to the new 4600, let's take a close look at the old 3800. You might be lucky enough to find one of these classics that is still rolling along. If so, here are a few tips on how to keep it in that happy condition.

The lubrication points are the wheel hubs, the chain, the pedal shaft, and the hinges and slides of the motor-engaging mechanism. One can of spray lube should last the lifetime of the machine. The rear brake (expanding drum type) is adjustable by a lever and in some models by a screw just behind the pedal on the left side of the frame. The front brake adjusts by means of a large knurled knob on the left of the steering yoke. Just push it in hard, twist to the left, release, and you have done a brake adjustment for yourself.

Because of its low compression and high proportion of oil to gasoline, coke builds up more quickly in the Solex than in other mo-peds and has a greater effect on performance. De-coking can be done in short-cut fashion by removing the intake-exhaust tubes and scraping the exhaust port and the inside of the exhaust tube, but it's best to take the cylinder off and do it right. Here's how:

Take off the gas tank, the fuel lines, the carburetor, and the intake-exhaust fitting. Remove the spark plug cover and take a good look at the compression-release mechanism as you're unscrewing the four head bolts. Solex has several variations of the compression-release device, all of them so simple that they're tricky to reassemble correctly on the first try.

Take off the aluminum head and look at all the carbon that's built up in its dome. Next, remove the four nine-millimeter nuts that hold down the cylinder and slip the barrel up over the piston. Don't break those piston rings! Parts for the Solex are hard to get. Cover the piston and the open crankcase with a rag, look in the port of the cylinder, and there you'll see the really heavy, constrictive buildup of coke that has so drastically diminished the performance of your old Solex. Work that eight-inch section of the exhaust tube out of the muffler pipe and get at the carbon with a little pick of some sort.

Chip away at it, and then scrape the steel clean. After you clean out that eight-inch tube, set cylinder and tube aside. Scrape the top of the aluminum piston more carefully, taking special care that the scrapings don't fall down into the crankcase. Take out the spark plug and clean it or replace it with a Champion L-85, work over the dome of the head, and turn your attention to the compression-release valve in the head.

If you have the special tool needed for refacing the valve seat, this important job can be done in a minute. Disassemble the valve keeper and spring, then slide the tiny poppet valve from the cylinder head. Lightly and carefully sand the valve stem free of carbon, then insert that special tool in the head and give it the few turns necessary to cut a new seat in the soft aluminum head.

If you don't happen to have that tool handy—and you won't since there are probably no more than fifty of them in the country—use valve grinding compound and work it between the valve and the seat, rotating the valve by means of the screwdriver slot in it. Now your Solex engine is all clean, and it can breathe once again when you've put it back together.

Use a little Permatex on the cylinder gasket if it's worn. There is no head gasket. Compress the piston rings with your fingers as you slide the cylinder down over the piston. Bolt it all down, including the head and the compression-release mechanism. Stick that eight-inch pipe back in place and screw on the intake-exhaust fitting. Take care in replacing the carburetor. There's a nylon gasket up inside the bottom of the carburetor that you're bound to overlook. Take it out and slip it over the intake tube before screwing that tube into the carburetor.

While the gas tank is off the motor, snug up the bolts that hold the side of the crankcase on. A machine that can vibrate the wallet out of your jeans can also work nuts and bolts loose now and then. You should tighten up the Solex nuts and bolts all around every month or two, and you should decoke it when it no longer pulls efficiently.

All assembled? Gas and oil right? Motor pushed down on the front wheel, choke moved to "start-depart" position, compression lever firmly depressed, start pedaling. Let go the compression-release lever—*pant, pant, pant—pft, pft, pft—putt, putt, putt—ahhh-h-h-h-h!*

A minor failing of the Solex is that its brake-throttle cable slips now and then, giving you even less control over the speed of the little thing and making you think you need decoking when you really don't. A seven-millimeter bolt on the carburetor holds the cable in place. Snug it up now and then.

And then there's the clutch. At idle it definitely drags, and without enough pedal assist it will wear out. It takes special tools to replace the clutch. Getting the flywheel off is the hard part, because it's a fairly fragile casting. Nine times out of ten, a standard wheel-puller will break the webbing on the casting. But there is a way to get it off.

You'll see three threaded holes on the mag-flywheel when you've taken off the plastic cover and the inspection plate inside it. And you'll see an acorn nut on the drive shaft. Find a big, heavy washer that covers the three holes and whose central hole just covers the hex head of the acorn nut. Drill the washer to fit the three holes, bolt it to the flywheel, and you'll have one of the special Solex tools. Just start unscrewing that acorn nut until its shoulder fits inside the washer's central hole. Keep on going, hard, and—pop!—the flywheel comes loose. That's the hard part.

It's even harder if you don't know how to keep the motor from turning over from the torque of the wrench. The Frenchmen have provided for this, too. There's an eight-millimeter bolt to the right of the fuel pump which doesn't hold anything on. All it does is open a hole to the crankcase, providing you with a means of sticking a stout awl or the handle of a file inside so that the crankshaft can't turn.

With the flywheel off, keep unscrewing and tugging at the works inside—and eventually you'll get to the clutch. A replacement clutch used to cost three bucks, but if you can't find that replacement, improvise with properly curved motorcycle brake shoes, an old leather belt, or whatever you can find that matches the shape of the worn shoes.

Want to set the timing? There's a mark on the flywheel and another on the back plate that says RUPTURE on it. The breaker points should be open to the thickness of a cigarette paper when the two marks come together.

And now that you've completely worked over your French granddaddy mo-ped, here's how it should stack up against a brand new Solex 4600:

Top speed	20 MPH
Fuel consumption	176 MPG
Front and rear suspension	none
Tires, front and rear	1.75 x 19
Compression ratio	8.2–1
Maximum engine speed	3800 RPM
Horsepower	0.7
Clutch	dry, centrifugal
Weight	62#, 28 kilograms
Length, wheelbase	39 inches, 1 meter

So who wants to buy a Solex? The clutch drags, and there's very little throttle play. Unlike other mo-peds, it won't start on the stand and run at idle while it warms up. It has no suspension, and running it over a rough road can void the warranty on your wristwatch. The kickstand is so narrow and the machine so top-heavy that the roar of a passing bus can send your Solex crashing to the parking lot blacktop. It's slow. Even an irate cocker spaniel can overtake you unless you find a handy downhill slope in a hurry. Parts and service are chancey.

On the other hand, it is a beautiful, classic machine. Thick paint, nice chrome trim, terrific tires, absolutely ingenious design. So it's slow, and you might have a dog problem—so what? You're stuck with a nice, leisurely pace, one which allows you to discover things in the neighborhood you never knew existed before. You can putt along on your Solex and have time to return the comments of pedestrians, then get on the pedals again and leave the walkers behind in a cloud of smiles.

The Solex is a great little machine: a classic in its time. It's best suited for people who want a lot of pedaling capability, and who have a short distance to travel with a long time to get there.

A mo-ped very similar to the Solex comes from Italy and is called the Bicizeta. Like the very early Solexes, the Bicizeta has a tubular frame. Performance is much the same as the Solex, including that top-heavy steering that takes a while to get used to. The big plus that the Bicizeta has is its breakaway feature. With the turn of a lever you can split your mo-ped in two, which makes for very handy storage at home and for great possibilities as a supplementary vehicle to be tucked under the bunk bed in the camper. The owners of small airplanes particularly like this feature in the Bicizeta, and it is a great convenience for the yachtsman pulling into a new seaport.

As ungainly as the Solex and Bicizeta mo-peds might look, these Cyclops machines were carefully designed. The frame was planned to take the motor while the motor was being planned to work with that particular frame.

Not so with the American front-wheel drive mo-ped, a device known as the Chicken Power. It looks as if it's built around an oversized model airplane motor, but it's a small chain saw motor which runs the Chicken Power's serrated steel roller. It looks as if it's fitted out with a beer can and a tuna fish can as part of the works, but those are the gas tank and the muffler, respectively. The parachute ripcord thing on the side is the recoil starter, like the one on your lawnmower. All these things are put together and placed in a box, along with instructions on how to attach it to the front of your bicycle.

In our opinion the Chicken Power isn't as good as the old Whizzer motorbike kit for two reasons. The Whizzer was specifically designed to make bicycles go, and the Chicken Power was not. The Whizzer was designed to fit on the standard bicycle of the day, a heavy-framed, balloon-tired, one-speed, while the Chicken Power is just too much for today's lightweight ten-speed. But it's a good gadget to invest in if you're more interested in tinkering than in mo-ped riding.

From the Solex to the Chicken Power, the front-wheelers are fun and different. But the far greater number of rear-wheel-drive mo-peds make it "the new wonder vehicle."

4 Ciao, Baby!

Ciao (chow) is Italian slang for hello, good-bye, hiya, so long, and whaddayasay. Ciao also happens to be the trademark for the fine little mo-ped that's made by the Piaggio Company of Genoa, Italy.

Though the Ciao is a relative newcomer to the mo-ped ranks, Piaggio is an old-time company, highly experienced in quality two-cycle engines and in super-economical vehicles. It started about a century ago, making ship fittings and hardware, and progressed through boats and airplanes and three-wheeled minitrucks. At the end of World War II it introduced a vehicle that's well known and highly regarded throughout the world as one of the most reliable, economical, unique, and fun two-wheelers ever made—the Vespa motorscooter.

You've seen them in European movies with a flashy-toothed guy seated behind the cowling and a mini-skirted girl sitting side-saddle behind him. You've seen them chugging along the American beach, badly rusted and bruised, lugging a surfer and his board. And you've seen them in TV scenes of Southeast Asia evacuations, carrying a whole family to safety. The worldwide acceptance of the Vespa motorscooter speaks volumes for its quality, and at least another complete book would be needed to cover its adventuresome exploits and its simple maintenance. It's been around a long time, but only after decades of experience with the scooter did Piaggio enter the growing mo-ped market.

About ten years ago Piaggio's engineers released the little machine they called the Ciao. Its delicate lines, coupled with its rugged reliability and its highly reputable background, quickly established the Ciao as one of the best of the mo-peds. With a global dealership network already established for the Vespa motorscooter, the Vespa Ciao enjoyed rapid distribution and acceptance. In spite of all the restrictive American highway laws, quite a few Ciaos came into this country.

Most of these early Ciaos were purchased as toys and not as practical transportation vehicles. Retired people went for them as clever little contraptions on which to chug around the community with a minimum of effort and noise. They liked to show off their little European novelty to their admiring fellow retirees, and they enjoyed giving their grandkids a ride now and then. They quickly learned about the practical side of their funny little mo-ped.

The mini-motorcycle was just the thing for mini-trips to the mini-market, for instance. It could be pedaled through retirement trailer parks where motor-driven cycles are prohibited because of their noise. It could be stuck on the

Where's the motor? The Ciao's understated design is a feature most people like.

back of the camper to be used as a lifeboat and an errand vehicle. These original purchasers of the Ciao quickly learned it was more than just a novelty. Nevertheless the Ciao didn't receive the quick American acceptance that it deserved. Like many another invention, it was ahead of its time in this country. Mere thousands were sold, most of which are still running strong, some of which may be available secondhand. If those older machines have had even reasonable care, they're still in good shape. They can be rusty and dusty, with bent spokes and twisted fenders, but still have thousands of miles left in them. A once proud and gleaming new Ciao may have fallen into a disreputable state of neglect, but it can't be counted out because it's a very rugged little machine with a superb motor, and because—like the Solex—it's a very simple machine.

Most mo-ped engines are piston-ported; the Ciao's is not. It has a rotary intake valve, nothing more than a small pocket formed into the crankshaft lobe that picks up a measured amount of gas-oil mixture from the carburetor with each and every revolution of the motor and delivers this fuel to the crankcase. This keeps the bearing surfaces cooler, enabling the Ciao to run for years and years on only a two-percent oil mixture, and it makes for smoother engine performance through low, medium, and high-engine speeds.

The rotary intake valve engine—not to be confused with a true rotary engine—is typical of Piaggio's integrity of design. It didn't take all that much more to make the rotary valve engine—just some precision machining on the crankcase and some precision casting on the crankshaft—but in keeping with its reputation for quality in all things, Piaggio went ahead and did it.

46

The firm also tucked away the motor in such an inconspicuous manner that it is all but invisible. People have been known to pass by a parked Ciao for weeks, then finally stop and seek out the owner and say, "I give up. Is it electric or gas or what? Where's the motor?"

Well, it's right there in front of the pedals where it should be, underneath the streamlined gas tank that doesn't look like a gas tank at all. Only the tip of its spark plug, a few cooling vanes, and an unobtrusive muffler give you a clue. That is the whole motif of the Ciao. While other mo-peds look like mo-peds or try to look like their big brother motorcycles, the little Ciao just looks like a Ciao.

If the Ciao pays any price for its sleek, understated design, it is that the motor is a little hard to get to for an overhaul or for major adjustments. In fact, you have to drop the whole engine just to change a set of breaker points or replace a condenser. The fact that this doesn't have to be done once in five or ten thousand miles is a big compensation, but the engine nevertheless does have to come out of the frame now and then and be put back in without the aid of a shoehorn.

The Ciao is one of the easiest of all mo-peds to start. Of course, it can be started on its stand. Push down the choke lever by the right pedal, hold down the handlebars to make sure the back wheel is off the ground, and then step down hard on the pedal. It should be running now, and very quietly. Let it warm up a few seconds, then twist the throttle control and the choke lever flips up, and you're ready to run. Some models have an ignition key in addition to the compression-release lever, and this key doubles as the headlight and tail-light switch.

If your Ciao is hard to start, your spark plug probably needs cleaning and gapping. This is easily done after removal with the spark plug wrench that comes in your tool kit. The kit is located in a small black plastic box to the rear of the luggage rack. Scrape off the accumulated deposits on the electrodes, brush them clean or clean them with solvent, and reset the gap to .019 inch, or to 0.5 millimeter. A little kit called Klean-A-Plug is handy for this, complete with gapper, file, and brush, all neatly packaged in a leakproof container of cleaning solvent.

There's also a thirteen-millimeter open-end wrench in your tool kit for the bicycle chain take-up. The chain is on the right side, under the plastic chain cover. The plastic cover comes off quickly with a 90° twist of the three plastic securing screws. The Ciao's take-up sprocket is bolted on the inside of the pressed steel frame, next to the spokes of the rear wheel. Loosen that thirteen-millimeter nut from the inside, swing the sprocket forward in its circular groove, and tighten it up when you have about ten or fifteen millimeters of play in the chain. Too much or too little play will damage the sprockets. Lubricate the chain by hitting it with a little WD-40 or equivalent.

Check the spokes for tightness and use a bicycle-spoke tightener on them periodically. Pre-1972 Ciaos had spokes with a smaller diameter, so pay particular attention to these if you're fortunate enough to pick up an older Ciao at a good price.

Under the plastic cover on the left side is the motor-drive belt. Piaggio opted for a rubber vee belt here instead of the usual second chain on a mo-ped. As could be expected,

The only chain on a Ciao is operated by the pedals. With its sturdy plastic covers removed, the Ciao demonstrates just how much can be packed into an eighty-pound machine.

there's a good reason for this. A major nagging problem with a full-fledged motorcycle is its chain. The motor churning around, accelerating and decelerating, whips and jerks that chain constantly, leading in turn to transmission and motor misadjustments. Though this isn't such a vital matter on a mo-ped because of its smaller motor and simple transmission, Piaggio nevertheless did away with the chain in favor of a belt that has some give to it. The belt is quieter, lasts for many years, doesn't need oiling, and has the elasticity needed to make things easier on the single-gear transmission. If it does stretch a little, it can be taken up by sliding the engine forward in its three mounts.

The belt drives a pulley whose shaft goes inside the rear hub to the transmission. On the left side, inside that plastic cover you've removed, is a flat-headed screw plug. Unscrew it every five hundred miles or so to be sure the transmission is topped off with ninety-weight oil. Every few thousand miles, take out the plug, tilt the mo-ped over on its side to drain it, and refill with new ninety-weight.

Also under the left side cover is the clutch, a round steel thing which might look rusty and dirty on the outside, and which might make a clattery noise now and then, but which takes hold and continues to do the job for a long time. It consists of two concentric steel cups, one to drive the machine, the other to start its engine. Three curved, cork-faced shoes swing outward by centrifugal force to turn the outer cup and its attached pulley and thus drive the belt. They're spring-loaded to swing back when the engine is at idle speed. You can burn these out by planting your feet firmly on the ground and revving up the motor, or by trying to make your Ciao climb a super steep hill without a little help from your feet. Under normal use, expect five or six thousand miles from these shoes.

Inside the clutch and beyond those three pads is another cup and two more pads. These are faced with a composition material and are sprung like the cork pads, but in reverse. When you turn the pedals and the back wheel fast enough, these two pads swing out to turn the engine over a few times, enough to get it started, and then retract on springs while the heavier driving shoes do their job. These starting pads are rarely if ever replaced.

While you're working with the clutch you'll notice three motor mounting bolts sticking out through the frame. One has a long, black lever on it. When your belt develops a little play, loosen the three ten-millimeter bolts and the rear muffler bolt, push down hard on the lever, and the engine will slide forward to where you can tighten down the bolts with little or no slack in the belt.

With the motor mounts loosened and with the nut that holds the clutch screwed off, the whole clutch comes right off. On the side of the mag-flywheel you'll see a semicircular rubber pad. Work that out with the help of a screwdriver and rotate the flywheel until the breaker points put in their appearance. There's a little notch in the points assembly that will help you adjust them to the proper 0.4 millimeter (.015 inch for those of you still resisting the onrush of the metric system). Loosen the screw, adjust with a screwdriver in the notch, and cinch up again. But it's rarely that the points have to be either adjusted or replaced.

With the two gray plastic side covers off, there's still

another plastic engine cover. It's black and serves double duty as an occasional footrest. One prominent cad-plated screw holds it in place. Take it off, and at the rear of the engine assembly you'll see a little black plastic box with three holes in it, not to be confused with a battery. Loosen its single screw, ease it back and off the carburetor, and pull it up and out. There's a piece of stainless steel mesh in it, about the size of a silver dollar, the air filter. Smudgy dirt on this can drastically cut down engine performance, so wash it in solvent, blow it dry, and put it back together again. Take special care in getting the mesh and the filter case perfectly aligned. The smallest of air intake leaks in a two-cycle engine can cause very sluggish performance. Every part of a mo-ped engine is designed to close tolerances, so even a pinhole leak in the intake or a loose muffler throws it out of balance.

If you've still got a problem, take off the air cleaner again and remove the carburetor for cleaning. To do this, shut off the gas cock and unscrew the gas intake on the carburetor, which also holds in the fuel filter. Loosen the two screws that hold the top of the carburetor in and ease out the carburetor slide from the carburetor. It looks as if everything is going to fly apart at this point, but have faith, you're doing the right thing. Ease the carburetor back off the intake port and up and out of your mo-ped.

It comes apart easily. Just two screws hold it together. Inside is the traditional float and needle valve and a single carburetor jet. Take it all apart, wash it all carefully in solvent, blow it dry, and reassemble it. Inspect the nylon gasket that fits over the intake port, and if it's scratched or gouged, replace it in order to eliminate those little air intake leaks that can cause so much trouble. Reassemble the carburetor and air filter and you've got yourself a smooth running machine once again.

Still sluggish? Incredible! Time for de-coking.

Carburetor and air filter off. Remove the muffler. Unhook the compression-release cable. Break the three or four electrical connections, making note of the color coding of the wires in case you're fortunate enough to be in a position someday to reassemble it all. Remove the pedal chain. Loosen the three motor mounts and take off the clutch and belt. Disconnect the spark plug, turn the motor so the cylinder head is vertically down, and work the whole thing around, this way and that, till the engine slips down and out of the frame.

Now you can replace points and condenser. And now you can de-coke on a comfortable work bench instead of squatting on the ground.

You can go farther. You can take off the flywheel and split the engine case and rebuild the motor completely, but we can't really recommend that. With only minimal care, an overhaul will never be needed. And if for some reason an overhaul is needed, have your dealer take care of it. It isn't all that expensive.

You should reach a top speed on the level of 27 miles per hour with your Ciao. It's rated at 168 miles per gallon, but around town you'll suffer along with only about a hundred and forty. You can get even more mileage by pushing the black button on the left rear hub, converting to pedal power only. Reconnect the motor to the wheel by depressing the silvered lever just behind the button.

The Ciao takes pennies and pints at the gas station instead of dollars and gallons.

The Standard Ciao has bicycle type suspension—that is, none at all except in the saddle. The Deluxe model has swing arm suspension in the front, and a spring-loaded seat post for the saddle. The Deluxe has a speedo and a steering yoke lock which the Standard doesn't have. Both use 2 x 17 tires, with 20 pounds per square inch in front, 35 psi in the rear. Baskets and racks are available as accessories, and the Ciao comes in just about every color imaginable.

Compression ratio	9–1
Horsepower rating	1.5
Weight	80#, 38 kgs
Wheel base	39 inches, 1 meter
Fuel capacity	3 U.S. quarts
Spark plug gap	0.5 mm, .019 in.
Recommended plugs	NGK B6FS, ND W20FS, Bosch W145T1
Point setting	0.4 mm (19° BTDC)

The Ciao is a splendid little machine. It's light, quiet, easy to start and to handle, it's rugged and dependable, and it's good-looking: a stylish machine that gives you all you could ask for in a mo-ped. You'll probably enjoy more trouble-free riding with the Ciao than with any other mo-ped made today.

5 The Little Dutchman

A European company with a long history of farsightedness was the next to have a shot at the American mo-ped market. After delivering tens of thousands of mo-peds throughout the world, Batavus-Intercycle made a quiet splash with their quiet mo-ped in the United States. Here's how it all began.

The company was started by an inventive Dutchman named Andries Gaastra. In 1904 Andries opened a little shop in the Netherlands to sell clocks, watches, and sewing machines. Although he enjoyed immediate success with these rather stationary devices, his real interest lay in a wild new invention called a bicycle. When they put chains on bicycles, Andries became a bike freak. He was soon importing and selling a good German bike called the Presto, and soon after that came out with his own bicycle, which he called the Batavus.

Expansion was the watchword for Batavus-Intercycle from the start. By the end of World War I Andries had moved his bicycle works from the old clock shop to a plating shop and had his two sons working with him in the business. They continued to expand, and they somehow managed to survive those Depression years when a complete Batavus bicycle was selling for four (that's right) dollars. By then Andries' son Gerrit was taking an ever more active role in the company as it began production of three-wheeled bicycles, some of which were equipped with a little motor. Andries' yearning for wheels had been passed on to his son, and it wasn't long before young Gerrit had designed and built his very own motorcycle. The company survived World War II, Gerrit took over the helm, and in 1948 committed the company to its future in motorbikes.

What began as a bicycle with a motor attached quickly evolved into a very functional motorized two-wheeler, with motorcycle suspension front and rear, and with a growing number of fans throughout the world. One of their greatest boosters was a Dutchman named Kroon, sixty-five years old, who rode a Batavus mo-ped to Baghdad and back, to Egypt, Morocco, and throughout the United States. The company continued to grow, ever expanding, and finding each new plant they built was not quite enough to keep up with the demand for their machines.

Pride of workmanship is a big factor with the Dutch. A standout in the Batavus is its excellent paint job and high quality electroplating. And as you walk around this handsome machine, admiring all the way, you'll notice that it looks appreciably more like a miniature motorcycle than it does a bicycle or even a mo-ped. The motor is quite visible, tilting upward, with the entire cylinder and head in view. To

The Batavus from Holland has a distinct motorcycle look. Owing to its sprocket ratios, it is speedier than many other mo-peds.

call further attention to the motor, there is a long, chrome-plated exhaust pipe that extends well past the rear hub. With this engine arrangement, and with the telescoping fork suspension, it takes only a glance to know that while the Batavus is a pretty little machine, it is here on business.

It is quiet running, with a top speed of close to thirty miles an hour, and gets somewhere around 130 miles to the gallon. While it is a true mo-ped in every way, it leans more toward the motorcycle in appearance and maintenance.

A "start lever" is needed to start the motor of the Batavus. It is on the left handle grip, and by pulling it you disengage the clutch. This allows you to pedal the rear wheel and transmission up to speed so that when the start lever is released, the engine comes to life. You use the choke along with it by pulling the trigger on the right handlebar.

You can start it on the stand or off, and once the engine is running for half a minute or so, you can release the choke lever and just go. Of course, if the engine is already warmed up, don't use the choke. This two-hand, two-foot starting operation takes a bit of coordination at first but soon it can be done in seconds. The arrangement does not, however, allow for easy pedaling as a straight bicycle.

Batavus and most other mo-ped makers issue a warning against running the engine for long periods of time at constant speed during the break-in period. You should take it especially easy during the first fifty miles or so in your mo-ped's travels so that the piston rings can properly seat and the bearing surfaces wear in. Even then your mo-ped won't be broken in completely, and will take several hundred miles of road work before it gives you optimum speed and mileage.

Breaking in a two-stroke engine involves the reshaping of its piston. The piston in a brand-new two-stroke motor is perfectly cylindrical, but in use it gradually takes on the shape of a barrel. This is normal wear and is necessary for good performance. It takes a micrometer to detect that barrel shape, but it has to be there for the two-stroke engine to run just right. This proper shape is accomplished by varying the engine speed during the break-in period. Once that proper shape is obtained, you'll know it because the engine will suddenly be running smoother and your mileage will shoot up by ten or twenty percent. This is true for all mo-ped engines, and for all two-stroke engines.

Batavus in particular goes a step farther in its break-in recommendations. It puts an oversized main jet in the carburetor so that the engine runs very rich on gasoline and oil at first. It further pampers the young engine by recommending that a five percent gas-oil mixture be used during the first fifty miles. The big jet and the oily mix insures a good break-in, as long as you don't run at constant speed. After fifty miles or so, you can change to the smaller jet provided in the tool kit and lean down your mixture of gas-oil to four percent.

The jet is easily changed by unscrewing the slotted brass hex head on the side of the carburetor, removing the little brass fitting on the end of it, and replacing it with the newer, smaller jet.

There's an idle adjustment screw on the carburetor and, of course, there's that wire mesh air filter and the intake muffler. Keep the filter clean by washing in solvent periodically, and always take care that the entire intake system is put together snugly and firmly, without the smallest air leak. The plastic tube on the intake muffler should be pointing upward when it's in place.

Once in a while your Batavus might run poorly—or not at all!—because of a piece of grit or road dirt that's gone through the fuel filter and into the carburetor to lodge in the main jet. That jet, tiny as it is, happens to be most important since all the fuel your mo-ped consumes passes through it. The smallest particle can cut your available fuel very drastically. Clean the jet by taking it out, washing in solvent, and blowing through it with a hand pump. Never, no never, use a piece of wire to clean the little orifice because the smallest of scratches can result in sloppy, uneconomical running.

When cleaning the air filter, take the time to clean the diaphragm valve as well. This is on the exit side of the carburetor, between the carburetor and the engine, and is more commonly known as a reed valve. It acts in much the same way as the reed on a saxophone. It allows the air-fuel mixture to pass on through to the crankcase in one direction only. It closes down with the reversal of pressure in the crankcase so your fuel mixture can't go squirting back into the carburetor. This is a small but most effective refinement over the straight piston-ported engine. Like the rotary intake valve we've seen on the Ciao, the reed valve helps in smoothing out engine performance at various engine speeds. Pure piston-porting is great for the racing engine because it produces the most power at high engine speed. But for the street machine, stopping and starting every few blocks, power distribution has to be better, and the rotary valve or the reed valve is the way to do the job.

The Batavus has a rubber vee belt plus two driving chains, one for the pedals and the other for the motor. The right side chain, the pedal chain, is always kept at the proper tension by means of an automatic chain tensioner. The motor chain on the left should be kept adjusted to no more than three quarters of an inch of *total* play. That is, ⅜ inch upward and ⅜ inch down from a center line. (That's one centimeter in each direction.)

If there's too much movement here, ease off on the rear axle nuts and move the entire rear wheel back by means of the two nut-keys situated at the end of the rear fork. Make sure that the rear wheel stays exactly in the center of the fork before tightening the axle nuts again. This adjustment is very much like the chain adjustment on a motorcycle and can be carried out in a few minutes. The rubber vee belt should be checked from time to time and adjusted for tension too. It should have about 3/16 inch (half a centimeter, five millimeters) of travel in it. Too much play causes slipping and lack of power, too little causes bearing wear.

Point setting is relatively easy on the Batavus. At least you don't have to take the motor out for it. Just remove the left hand engine cover and there they are. The point gap is from .012 to .016 inches (0.3 to 0.4 millimeters), and the timing setting is 2.0 to 2.2 millimeters before top dead center. Happily, you'll rarely if ever have to adjust the breaker points or clean them or replace them or set the timing. The Batavus, like all mo-peds, is made to operate and enjoy, not to sweat and get greasy over. Concern yourself, if you will, with the more routine maintenance problems, and leave the major overhauls up to your authorized dealer.

These routine maintenance jobs are as follows:

- Clean that carburetor now and then, in particular the air filter and the main jet. When your clutch starts to drag, adjust the idler jet on the left side of the carburetor, screwing it out to slow down the motor to a speed where the clutch ceases to drag and turn the back wheel, screwing it in to keep the motor running at a comfortable idle speed.
- After fifteen hundred or two thousand miles, decarbonize the muffler and exhaust port and the cylinder head. Just remove the muffler, scrape off the carbon from around the exhaust port—taking care not to gouge the piston with your scraper—and scrape out the carbon caked in the muffler. Take off the head and do the same.
- Pay some attention to the spark plug every five hundred miles. Clean it, reset the gap to .020, and replace it.
- Keep the two chains oiled lightly and adjust the motor chain every five hundred miles. Check the auto tensioner on the pedal side for cleanliness and workability. WD-40 or any light oil will do nicely.
- Squirt some WD-40 into the cable housings every thousand miles, or whenever the cables to the brake, throttle, choke, and so on seem as if they're starting to bind. There's nothing more frustrating than a broken throttle cable twenty miles from home. There's a special grease fitting on the speedometer drive that will gratefully accept a drop of oil from you every fifteen hundred miles.
- Tighten up the nuts and bolts all around every five hundred miles, and while you're at it, grease the nipple on

Dad can buzz to work on a mo-ped with very little danger of acquiring the chopper-rider image.

the pulley via the grease fitting. Before you grease or oil anything, wipe away the accumulated road dust to keep from squirting that abrasive junk in along with the lubes.

• If the front fork squeaks, shoot it with oil. Pack the steering head and pedals with grease every five hundred miles. Don't worry about the axle bearings or the swing-arm bearings, as these are self-lubricating.

• The clutch-cable lever should have 3/16 inch (five millimeters) of play before it engages, or else excessive wear will develop. Batavus has thoughtfully provided you with a clutch adjustment right there at your left hand. Just ease off on the knurled lock nut, turn the knurled adjusting screw so that you have that all-important five-millimeter clearance, and tighten down the lock nut again. The hand brakes have the same sort of adjustment. About an inch of play is comfortable here before the brakes cinch down.

Take care of the little Dutchman and he'll take care of you. Some of the regular maintenance checkouts and greasings might sound a bit tedious to you, but if Kroon could make it to Morocco on his Batavus, you can at least keep the spark plug in order.

The Batavus has a wheel base of 42 inches and it weighs 106 pounds. It's Laura engine has a displacement of 48 cubic centimeters, and it drives you along on the level at close to thirty miles per hour. It has front and rear telescoping suspension, which makes for a very soft, comfortable ride. It comes in orange or violet.

The Batavus is a good machine, a nice, rugged mo-ped with a comfortable ride and a pretty good top speed. It has a racy look that will appeal to the sportsman in you, and it will reliably get you over a hundred and thirty miles around town on a gallon of gasoline.

6 A Hundred Million Frenchmen

Paris teems with mo-peds. You'll see them at every turn there, parked before the sidewalk cafés and outside Le Drugstore, ripping up and down the Rue de la Paix, crashing together under the Arc de Triomphe. They are used for delivery vehicles and for commuting, and just about every Parisian teenybopper has his or her own mo-ped for the personal freedom needed with which to grow up. These little machines typify the Gallic attitude of freedom and independence in all things, without making any concessions to European frugality.

Paris is a virtual museum of functioning mo-peds of every age, representing every one of the over forty different brands available in Europe. Absolutely antiquated mo-peds challenge aggressive taxicabs for rights of way, and mo-peds new and old vie with each other constantly for advantage on the road. Solexes abound, Italian and German and Dutch machines blithely mingle in putt-putting, pedaling hordes, and through these masses of beeping velocipedes the

69

Cadillac of the mo-ped world proceeds upon its stately way, the Rolls-Royce of the motorbikes takes its proud place in the pack, the Peugeot cruises on.

Ardent bicycle fans will argue the merits of the Peugot bicycle. It has weaknesses, they say, in comparison to the English and the Japanese ten-speeds, and most of these weaknesses seem to be in a certain slowness in keeping up with modern changes in the bicycle, a certain clinging to past glories. The Peugeot people manufacture a good, solid extends to the Peugeot mo-ped as well—except that while the Peugeot bicycle is merely good, the Peugeot mo-ped is superb.

Compared to the other little street bikes, the Peugeot is a superb.

Compared to the other little street bikes, the Peugot is a real aristocrat. It comes in four basic models. And with optional sprocket changes, these four extend to at least twenty different machines, more than enough to satisfy any mo-pedaling needs. Though most mo-peds get wavery and sluggish while carrying an extra passenger, the Peugeot 104 comes with a buddy seat as standard equipment. White sidewall tires are standard on several of the Peugeot models, and Peugeot extends the range of its machines with integral auxiliary gas tanks. Its service manuals are elegantly illustrated and about as highly detailed as those for a Honda 750. Some models have variable speed transmissions and all models look as sleek and quietly expensive as they truly are. The Peugeot is deservedly the snob of the mo-ped world, as exemplified by this opening passage, lifted word for word from the owner's manual:

Dear Madam, dear Sir!

I am the PEUGEOT mo-ped, one of the most reliable assistants you can dream of.

I thank you for having selected me, and I am very glad to be in your hands today.

I have the best intentions. Not only will my clean lines be a credit to your taste, but, above all, I have decided to do the most for you. Thanks to me the journey to your work as well as your holidays will be carefree and pleasant for you.

However, if you want our relationship to remain perfect, read these few pages carefully thought up for you by my makers, particularly the hints about my routine maintenance. Please follow these in order to keep me always like new.

I am expecting you for our first trip. . . .

This sort of vanity is quite in order with the Peugeot, for the machine appeals to a different individual than the average mo-ped.

The Peugeot is for the rich kid, and even more for the gaberdine-suited businessman commuting within the city limits of Paris. It's in a class by itself, which is exactly what that Parisian businessman wants, lest he be identified too closely with the hordes of younger mo-pedalers ripping around on the cobblestoned streets without a care in the world. It's a great machine, very quiet and quite fast for a mo-ped. It's built to last for years and years. For prestige, elegance and solid comfort, get yourself a Peugeot—but don't get one if you're an unmechanical type who's living out in the boondocks.

It's the same old story. Buy yourself a Jaguar and it will

run beautifully for years. But if a generator or bearing goes bad, you're out of wheels unless you live close to a service center. Buy a Volkswagen, and though it's not quite as smooth as a Jag, it will run forever because you can always get spare parts for it, no matter where you are, and you can usually install those spare parts yourself. Treat your Peugeot like a Jag or a Caddie and it will do well by you.

During the running-in period, use an eight-percent oil-gas mixture. After about sixty-five miles, drop it down to six percent. Fire up your Peugeot either by pedaling it off down the boulevard or by tromping down on the pedal while it's on the stand. In either case, you give it a little gas, pull the choke lever in, pull the compression lever in, and release the right-hand compression lever just as the engine gets up to starting speed. Hold the choke on for a while longer, especially during colder weather. Use the decompression lever to stop the engine.

There's a wire lever on the pedal pulley, a different sort of configuration for the one-speed and for the variable-speed transmission models. Depress this to convert your Peugeot to pure pedal power, but don't expect it to pedal as easily as a ten-speed. There are grease fittings on the pedal pulley and clutch which should be squirted every thousand miles, and the chains and the control cables should be oiled every six hundred or seven hundred miles.

Peugeot recommends that the wheel bearing cups, the telescoping forks be lubed every 6,250 miles—at one of their service stations. Peugeot trusts you, the owner of their proud machine, to adjust the height of the seat and the handlebars, but they urge you to take the machine to their dealer for decarbonizing somewhere after 3,100 miles. It suggests that its BP-ZOOM 2-stroke oil be used in order to extend the life of the machine between decarbonizings. Rubber vee belt tensioning is another job to be performed by your serviceman, but the two drive chains may be adjusted by the owner with the turn screws on the rear hub.

In case of engine trouble, Peugeot suggest that you might have run out of petrol. Plenty of petrol? Then perhaps the petrol filter or the vent hole in the gas cap is clogged, or the carburetor jet is dirty. Since the Peugeot comes equipped with a tire pump, you can blow the carb and filter clean once you've taken it apart. Still got troubles? Clean, reset, and dry off the spark plug, and if your troubles persist, "In case all the above mentioned checks give no satisfactory results, the mo-ped must be taken to the dealer or to the nearest agency for an overhaul."

Great machine, the Peugeot. It is the Cadillac, the Rolls-Royce of the mo-ped world. If you're out for top quality and prestige, and still after the fun of a mo-ped, head for your Peugeot dealer.

And then there is Motobecane: a great name in bicycle racing, universally known in the mo-ped world as maker of the Mobylette. Motobecane started out as manufacturer of the first French lightweight motorcycle some time in the twenties in a little shop just outside Paris. It claims the mo-ped it introduced in the Paris Motorcycle Show in 1949 became the Model T of the mo-peds. While in our opinion the Solex holds this honor, the Motobecane remains a fine, basic, time-honored machine.

It was Motobecane who first introduced the double-acting automatic clutch that has been so widely copied by other mo-ped makers. This is two circular clutches in one housing, with the first coming into play with the speed of the rear wheel, then engaging the second to turn over the engine till it starts, whereupon the first clutch retires from action until such time as the rider wants to start his engine again.

The Motobecane is a quality machine, with chrome-plated cylinders, sturdy construction, good finish. The engine is very visible; there is no way of mistaking the Motobecane for anything but a motorized bicycle. It's made to ride, and since it has a motorcycle heritage, its makers realize that it can have a problem now and then and they give clear and concise maintenance instructions and suggest you consult your dealer only "if in doubt." Since the Motobecane, like any other mo-ped, is a mechanical contrivance, there's no doubt that at some time in your relationship with it you will have some trouble with it. And there's no doubt that in most cases you can fix whatever's wrong with it yourself.

You start it up by the same two-handed procedure used with the Peugeot—choking and decompressing simultaneously, getting that piston to move by means of the pedals, then letting go of the compression-release lever. It's a process that sounds much more complicated than it is, and that soon becomes second nature. Brakes and controls are in the standard places on the four different models of Motobecane, and there's the standard type tool kit under the seat post, plus a tire pump clipped under the gas tank. The seat and handlebars are adjustable up and down.

It has a gas tank capacity of 0.8 gallon, including the reserve supply, and its piston-ported engine calls for a four-percent mixture of two-stroke oil in the gas. The manufacturers have thoughtfully packaged a good grade of this oil in four-ounce tubes, just enough to take care of one tankful of gasoline and keep you going when you've switched on to reserve.

Once again we have a machine with a rubber vee belt for its primary drive, plus two chains for delivering the driving force to the rear wheel. Although it seems a little complicated, it's not really a bad arrangement, as Motobecane has proved with the millions of mo-ped miles racked up on its tough little machine. The vee belt and the motor-drive chain are disengaged for pedaling like a straight bicycle by a lever on the vee belt's front pulley. It's a rather heavy machine to pedal, but it zips right along on its motor, with a minimum of pedal assist on the hills.

Its makers expect you to ride their product a lot, and at six-hundred-mile intervals to use some thirty-weight oil on the brake-lever pivot bolts, the brake-cable nipples, the decompressor lever and its cable. While you're at it, oil the choke lever and cable, the throttle and speedo cable, the pedals and the kick stand. These are all common sense oiling points and shouldn't be neglected if you expect to get the most out of your Motobecane.

At the same intervals, squirt some grease from a gun into the four grease fittings on the clutch, the kick stand pivot spindle, the drive belt pulley shaft, and the telescoping front forks. The very fact that Motobecane has provided these grease fittings is a commentary on how they want you to keep your machine going for a long time. Only after 3,600 miles are on your odometer do they suggest you return your Motobecane mo-ped to your dealer, where he can check it out a bit and grease the bearings at the front and rear hubs and on the steering head.

It's better, however, to get any mo-ped back to its point of origin much sooner, at something like five hundred miles. By then you're pretty familiar with your bike, you might have some further questions about its operation, and you're better qualified to benefit from what your dealer tells you about it.

Of course, pay some attention to your Motobecane's chains. Oil with fifty-weight every six hundred miles, and keep the tension adjusted to half to three quarters of an inch with the adjusting screws on the rear hub. They are quick acting, in the motorcycle fashion. If you take a jaunt through Death Valley or buzz through the Sahara Desert and get your chains in a particularly deplorable condition, take them right off, wash them in solvent, and hang them up to dry with the Monday morning wash. The pedal-chain tensioner, by the way, only needs adjustment on the 40TS and 40TL models, with the 50S and 50L models having an automatic tensioner.

All the cable adjustments are right there on the handlebars, so conveniently situated that brakes and all the rest of it may be adjusted while you're in motion. It's best to stop, however, and get off to adjust the carburetor on your Motobecane.

The carburetor is under the left side cover. There's a little screw right at the intake manifold that adjusts your idling speed. This should be kept adjusted so that the engine runs at the slowest comfortable speed, well short of a speed that would engage the clutch and turn the rear wheel. The main jet is directly underneath the idle adjustment screw. Take it out and clean it with solvent and an air stream if you suspect dirty fuel as a cause for erratic engine performance, or if too much choking is needed to get your Motobecane buzzing.

There's a plastic mesh fuel filter on top of the carburetor and another in the fuel tap. Make sure they haven't filtered out so much gasoline junk that they're no longer passing any gasoline. As always, make sure all the fuel intake system is firmly tightened up to prevent any air leaks.

The top speed of the Motobecane varies with the model and is anywhere from twenty–thirty miles per hour.

Best fuel consumption	148 MPG
Front suspension	telescoping
Rear suspension depends on the model, either solid or swing-arm.	
Tires	2.00 x 17 or 2.25 x 17
Compression ratio	7.8–1
Horsepower rating	1
Maximum engine speed	3800 RPM
Weight	98#, 44 kg
Wheel base, depending on model	45–48 inches
Overall length	66 to 69 inches
Point setting	.016 inch or 0.4 mm
Ignition timing setting	1 mm BTDC

Your Motobecane will come equipped with a fork lock, a

tool kit, tire pump, with baskets and saddle bags and luggage racks available as accessories. Turn signals are not available from the factory but may be added by the owner.

The Motobecane is a good, solid machine, with emphasis on lots of use during a long lifetime. It has a very low compression engine to extend that lifetime. It's a relatively heavy mo-ped and rather a long one. It isn't as quick as some of the other machines, but it will last for many years without problems and with a lot of solid riding comfort.

7 The International Machine

Mo-peds are manufactured in Italy, France, Holland, Austria, Germany, and Belgium, making the handy little machine truly international.

Belgium's offering in this field of individualized transportation is the Flandria. Even at a distance it can hardly be mistaken for any other mo-ped because of its boxy headlamp and the distinctive sweeping lines of its gas tank. The frame is a combination of tubular steel and pressed steel, suspended with telescoping forks front and rear on the Suburbia model of the Flandria and in front only on the cheaper Collegiate model. On both models, a rubber vee belt plus two chains provide the driving force. Front and rear wheels are covered with wraparound fenders best suited for Belgium's rainy weather.

The Flandria has comfortably large handlebars and a gas tank that holds more than a gallon of four percent oiled fuel. Its engine's relatively low compression ratio of 7.5 to 1 makes for long engine life. Its makers claim 2.1 horse power and, depending on the model, a dry weight of from ninety-two to ninety-seven pounds. Buddy seats and baby seats are available as options, and its strong piston-ported engine and tough frame make for good operation even under a heavy load. They also make for gasoline consumption which isn't spectacular, but still not bad.

A. Claeys is the manufacturer. This company makes a large variety of two-wheelers, all of them in the forty-nine cubic centimeter class, most of them with multi-speed transmissions instead of pedals. The company manufactures its own motor, a solid little affair that's easy to work on and quite durable. To make the motor last even longer, adjust the drive chain on your Flandria every 250 miles. It should have about ten millimeters of overall up and down play in it to operate best. And when you're adjusting the chain, check the engine oil lever at the filling plug on the left side of the engine case. Top it off with thirty-weight oil if it's low, and change the oil there every thousand miles.

After you've put your first 500 miles on your Flandria, it's time to check the telescoping suspensions and to tighten and lubricate the cables all around. The steering bearings should also be inspected and lubed every thousand miles. In addition to these maintenance points there remains the routine spark plug inspection and cleaning and adjustment and the bicycle type maintenance, spoke tightening and chain lubrication.

The Flandria is a good machine, especially if you want a heavy duty mo-ped that can carry a passenger short distances in relative comfort. As you would do in the selection of any mo-ped, satisfy yourself that your particular dealer plans to stay in operation so that you can get spare parts as you need them. A four-hundred-dollar machine that's out of service for want of a twenty-five-cent part is not the best transportation bargain available.

The Puch is made in Austria. It's been a famous name in European cycling over the years, a mo-ped with a proven history of reliability. Years ago Sears Roebuck scoured the world for a mo-ped to go along with its Vespa-Allstate motorscooter and finally selected the Puch as the machine to bear its trademark. The Allstate-Puch of several years ago was a heavy and rather cumbersome machine. This has evolved into the modern Puch, a handsome, streamlined two-wheeler that's sure to succeed in pleasing the American who's interested in stylish, low-cost transportation.

The American version of the Puch is offered in several models, all with speeds of less than thirty miles per hour. They weigh in at about eighty-five pounds, and they burn up a gallon of gasoline-oil mix for every 147 miles they travel under ideal conditions. Their twenty-one inch tires are slightly larger than the average in mo-peds, and they come equipped with a tire pump as a standard accessory.

Use four percent of two-cycle oil in the gasoline your Puch consumes. Use automatic transmission fluid in the gearbox, changing this fluid every two thousand miles. As with the Batavus, the main jet in the carburetor should be replaced with the factory supplied smaller jet after the first 300 miles of break-in operation. Puch has a selection of several jets from which to choose. The ideal one for your particular altitude and general riding conditions can best be found through trial and error, or by checking with your dealer.

Starting with the standard main jet, test ride your Puch, then again with the next larger and the next smaller jets while you check your top speed with the speedo or with a stopwatch. The best jet for you is the one that gives you slightly less than top speed. There's an air mixture needle adjustment on the Puch's Bing carburetor that can be adjusted to give you optimum performance at low and at moderate engine speeds, but this adjustment has no effect on top speed.

If your carburetor is running too lean—too much air in the mixture—the engine will ping and overheat, and could cause a piston seizure as well, in time. Too rich a mixture will cause spark plug fouling and sloppy, irregular engine performance. Idle speed adjustment is done right there on the left side of the carburetor by means of the slotted screw.

If it ever becomes necessary, ignition timing is not much of a chore on the Puch. Set the timing at from sixteen to eighteen millimeters against the operating direction on the circumference of the flywheel from top dead center. Breaker points gap should be from .014 to .018 inch, and if this gap setting is changed, the timing should be reset as well. If you replace the points, replace the condenser at the same time.

Some mo-peds don't have provisions for such things as timing setting and carburetor jet changing as the Puch

The Puch offers highly economical and convenient transportation ideal for running around town.

has. Don't let this seemingly more complex situation scare you away from the Puch. It's something that very rarely has to be done, and it sounds more complex than it is. Of course, it's something that can be done by the dealer, but on the other hand you can learn a lot from owning and working on your Puch yourself. It's a fine machine, able to run for years with a minimum of service. Those measures they've provided for ignition and fuel adjustments are there more as a bonus than as a necessity.

The Germans can be counted on to keep up with anyone when it comes to motor-driven vehicles. Their Autobahn is an ideal roadway for their Mercedes-Benz and Volkswagen automobiles, and the streets of Berlin are just as ideal for their Kreidler mo-ped.

Kreidler is a big name there in small motors with high performance. A highly modified Kreidler mo-ped once hit over a hundred miles an hour over a well-prepared straightaway, with the assistance of a lot of gears. The standard, road-ready Kreidler mo-ped features two gears in its automatic transmission, but its top speed is under thirty miles per hour, in keeping with mo-ped standards.

It's not a bad-looking machine. It looks a little Teutonic with its chromed gas tank and muffler, but it has a nice, solid design appearance. There's a telescopic suspension front and rear, plus swing arm suspension in the back. It has two driving chains, one for pedals, one for motor, both concealed under plastic side covers. It's a standard mo-ped with its only departure from the norm being that automatic, two-speed transmission. The handlebars seem a little small, but they do the job. Access to the engine is easy for cleaning

Germany's Kreidler mo-ped features a two-speed transmission—automatic, of course—plus lots of chrome.

the extra large intake muffler and wire mesh air filter, and for making carburetor and ignition adjustments.

The Kreidler weighs 106 pounds, lays a claim to getting a hundred and fifty miles per gallon, and has the standard two-stroke engine of forty-nine cubic centimeters. This engine calls for a five percent oil mix. It's nice and quiet, and it caters to the German taste for comfort. The two-speed transmission is a rather elegant feature, operating so smoothly you hardly know it's there. Although this does add some complexity to the Kreidler, don't expect it to add any maintenance problems.

With the exception of the front-drive Bicizeta, most mo-peds rely on pressed steel for their frames. This is good construction, perfectly ample for a mo-ped, and it allows for making the gas tank as an integral part of the frame. Pressed steel also makes for latitude in design that allows for making the gas tank an integral part of the Tube steel, however, is a stronger method of constructing a frame, and with an inventive designer on the payroll you can have your pleasing appearance and still enjoy the stronger construction of tubular steel. Cimatti of Italy has done this with their City Bike. It's powered by the time-tested Minarelli engine, and it has the look and the feel of that practicality and quality in motor vehicles for which the Italians are world-renowned.

The City Bike looks solid enough to stand up through a couple of Baja 1000 races. Its departure from the mo-peds' traditional pressed steel frame has moved the rather small gas tank back over the rear fender, and it looks as if that's exactly where the tank belongs. More tubular steel protects the tank and at the same time makes up a very sturdy luggage rack. The City Bike's designers had sturdiness in mind throughout when they put the machine on the drawing board, but still they managed to come up with those distinctively sleek Italian lines.

There's telescoping suspension front and rear in the City Bike, plus swing-arm suspension in the rear. It has heavy tires, somewhat smaller than those of the average mo-ped, with wraparound fenders affording maximum protection on wet roads. Its Minarelli motor is a highly respected one, and it's equipped with an oversized muffler that keeps its noise level at an absolute minimum. Unlike most other mo-peds, it has only a single chain to drive it. This is made possible by placement of the pedal shaft directly through the motor case, eliminating the front sprocket entirely at the expense of making the engine works only slightly more complicated.

The City Bike is fired up like most others, on or off the stand, using a clutch lever instead of a compression release. This lever looks and acts just like a compression release lever, but it doesn't work that way. It will not, for instance, stop the motor once it's running. The City Bike has a kill button for this, located on top of the light control switch, which grounds out the spark plug.

Cimatti recommends a 600-mile break-in period, which speaks well for their regard for their machine's long life. Change the oil in your City Bike after the first 150 miles by draining through the plug on the very bottom of the engine case. Refill with twenty-weight oil through the larger plug located just above the pedal shaft, adding oil until it runs out through the check point plug directly underneath the pedal shaft. After this break-in oil is changed, change it again every 1,500 miles. During the period of break-in, pamper your City Bike a bit by keeping its speed under twenty-five miles per hour, and by avoiding really steep hills, and making sure your gasoline-oil mix is five percent. You can cut down to four percent after this.

The single chain on the Cimatti has adjusters on it of the quick-acting motorcycle type, eccentric disks that are held in place by nuts on each side of the rear axle. Loosen the nuts and turn the adjusters evenly to ensure straight rear wheel alignment and to keep the play of the chain at about half an inch. For best mileage and most comfort, keep the tire pressures at 21.5 and 35.5 psi front and rear respectively.

The front fork, steering bearings, and rear axle should be greased periodically. This entails a good deal of disassembly and delving into the innards of the machine. The front wheel and fender have to come off to grease the forks, which is a nuisance. The handlebars have to come off for bearing inspection and greasing, and the rear wheel for greasing the rear axle. Cimatti designers could have made these maintenance items a little easier, it seems, but once again, they're not something that must be done every day.

Special tools are called for to overhaul the Minarelli engine, but these can be improvised if you're in a jam for a new piston or bearings. The timing on the Minarelli motor isn't rigidly set as it is in most other mo-peds and can be altered by rotating a plate that holds the points and condenser. Timing marks on the engine case make this a simple enough operation once you've done it a few times,

The all tubular frame of the Cimatti City Bike sets it apart from other mo-peds. Its Minarelli motor is a fine one.

but really, all you'll ever need to do, most likely, is to keep the spark plug gapped to .024 inch and the points set at from .014 to .018 inch. Timing setting is 23° before top dead center. It's set at the factory like this, and if it ever becomes necessary to remove the timing plate, make a scribe mark beforehand to align the plate to the engine case upon reassembly. Cimatti suggests their dealer do the timing for you as well as the carburetor adjustments and brake inspections. You can do the rest, if you wish, guided by the owner's manual.

At 105 pounds the City Bike is a little on the heavy side, but you don't notice it in driving. It has mechanical features usually seen only in more sophisticated machines, such as its fan-cooled motor and its classy Dell'Orto carburetor. It turns out a respectable 1.9 horsepower, and it can be counted on to give the same good service in American cities as it has throughout Europe.

Even the gypsy nation has its representative in the mo-ped world. Gitane is the word for gypsy in Spanish and French, and the little Gitane mo-ped is just the ticket for carefree wandering on country roads or city streets. It is made in France, and is another machine powered by the well built and reliable Minarelli 49.6-cc two-stroke motor. The engine has an eight-to-one compression ratio operating on a five-percent oil mix, and can turn out 7,000 RPM at top speed.

The Gitane holds one and a half gallons of gasoline and can get up to 175 miles to the gallon. It weighs just over a hundred pounds, and it has telescoping suspension front and rear, plus swing-arm suspension in the rear. This is probably more than it needs in the way of spring action and

The Gitane's telescoping suspension, front and rear, takes the bumps out of the road.

shock absorption, but it does provide a good soft ride. White sidewall tires are standard on this sporty machine.

This is another mo-ped that requires a minimum of periodic maintenance. The swing arms and the wheel bearings need greasing and adjusting every 6,000 miles. Air cleaner should be checked and cleaned, if necessary, every 1,000 miles. Gitane's makers recommend checking the breaker points every 1,500 miles and cleaning and adjusting them every 4,000 miles. They suggest the points be polished with carborundum stone, silicone carbide paper, or very fine emery cloth, and afterwards cleaned with alcohol or gasoline.

We respectfully disagree with this procedure. If your breaker points are dirty or worn, simply replace them. Once breaker points are cleaned, polished, or sanded, they are never the same. With only one spark plug in your machine, you need a good hot spark each and every time the engine fires, and the prerequisite for this is good, clean breaker points. You need breaker points with flat, parallel surfaces, and those surfaces aren't always so flat once you've used fine sandpaper on them. Our advice is to forget about the breaker points until such time as your mo-ped's motor is truly faltering, and then to adjust them to the manufacturer's standards if they are not already there. But if they're dirty or worn, replace them. It is really no more of a job than it is to file or sand them, new points only cost three or four dollars, and when you're done with the job you're certain your points are good.

The Gitane starts on the stand or off, with the aid of a clutch control lever. Depress the lever under your left hand

and pedal till the engine is up to speed, then release the clutch control lever and your engine is running. Choke it, of course, when the weather is cold.

One of our favorite features about the Gitane is its single chain, and the easy acting chain adjusters. Adjust the chain carefully. There should be fifteen to twenty millimeters of travel in the chain once it is properly adjusted. Have a look at it once every week, and adjust it as necessary. The Gitane ranks as one of the chain-driven mo-peds that does not require much maintenance.

8 The Electric Mo-Ped

The idea of an all-electric vehicle is absolutely intrigue-ing. It is noiseless. It does not pollute the atmosphere. Plug it into the wall each night and refuel it for only pennies. Or attach a bank of solar cells to it so the sun recharges your batteries as you ride. Or hook up a windmill-generator to it to do the same. Every one of these concepts stir the imagination, but at this point in man's technology, they just don't work out.

Take the wind-driven battery charger. You cruise along at thirty miles per hour and the slipstream created by your vehicle turns the fans of a windmill that revolves your generator to keep your batteries charged as they power the motor that turns your wheels. It sounds as clean and simple as can be, and people have labored over similar conceptions for centuries, and the concept is quite impossible. It's called perpetual motion, and it involves creating energy out of nothing, and that just can't be done.

How about the solar-cell idea? That is at least within the

realm of possibility, but it would take a bank of solar cells the size of a gigantic beach umbrella to move a bicycle sized vehicle at even a snail's pace, and the cost would be astronomical.

You could, however, recharge an electric vehicle's batteries through a standard wall outlet for not very many pennies. First, however, you've got to buy those batteries, and batteries big enough to move themselves and you along at twenty or thirty miles an hour cost a lot of pennies. Once the batteries are paid for, there's the battery charging circuit to feed DC current to them, and the wall outlet, and the wires to that outlet, all the way back to the power generating station. Electricity is cheap, but it's not free, especially when you're planning on carrying it around with you. Electricity is cheap, but in the end its price is tied to that of petroleum products, and it is not going to get any cheaper in our lifetimes.

"But," you say, "I can afford to pay for the batteries and the charger and the wires and the electricity, especially since my all-electric vehicle does not pollute." Maybe that vehicle doesn't pollute, but the generating station does. Most of them are still powered by petroleum products or by coal. Others produce electricity by means of huge dams to trap the energy in rivers, and still others convert nuclear power to electricity, with heat pollution as a by-product. Nuclear power and someday solar generating stations will provide the power in the future, but to date electricity costs money and creates its own, more subtle forms of pollution.

But the electric vehicle, the electric mo-ped, is indeed noiseless, and it does have its place in the scheme of things, and it is available.

96

The Solo Electric from Germany typifies most electric vehicles with unusual lines built around lots of batteries.

The Solo Electra is made in Germany, and it looks much as you'd expect an electric mo-ped to look. It's short and squatty, with high-rise handlebars and doughnut fat wheels. It's built quite well, with a tubular steel frame and stainless steel fenders and an adjustable saddle. Hand throttle and hand brakes make the Solo Electra go and stop, and there's a dial ammeter to tell you when you're drawing a lot of power from the batteries and when you're cruising along at minimum power consumption. And there's a big, stream-lined plastic box, around which the whole machine is built, which holds those big batteries.

Half the weight of the Solo Electra is in batteries, and those batteries can move you and your machine along at sixteen miles per hour for about twenty-five miles before they need recharging. There's a good deal of wiring, solenoids, controls, and circuitry that goes along with the batteries, plus the charging system that usually stays at home. All this runs up the cost as well as the weight of the machine. It has a two-speed transmission and automatic clutch, one vee belt and chain, a speedometer and odome-ter, plus that charging indicator that keeps reminding you that soon you've got to turn around and head for the socket. It has pedals too, which makes it a mo-ped, but the Solo Electra isn't an easy machine to make move with your feet.

However, the Solo Electra works. It's a novel pleasure to operate, and it will draw stares and praise to you for your sincere and obviously expensive effort toward being a non-gasser. But for real, day-to-day use as a transportation machine, the Solo Electra doesn't yet measure up to the conventional gasoline-powered mo-ped.

There are other electric motor vehicles around. Each has its limitations. One of them is a true mo-ped.

An American aerospace engineer from Southern California designed it. He took an ordinary bicycle and fitted it out with batteries and a pair of electric motors, and it worked. An early prototype of his machine consisted of a rather heavy three-speed bike to which the motors had been bolted, and a pair of very heavy, twelve-volt automobile batteries hanging down from the rear axle on brackets. The driving motors worked together against the rear wheel, providing evenly distributed pressure against both sides of the tire casing, well away from the tread surface. You got up a little speed by pedaling, hit a handlebar switch, and the two motors went to work in synchronization to boost you along at ten or fifteen miles an hour, without the slightest bit of noise or effort. It was a great little invention, but this early prototype didn't look very graceful, and it was hard to get up over curbs because the batteries weighed about forty pounds apiece.

It did work, however, and it encouraged further development of this electric mo-ped to a point where it's in production today. The motors look sleek now. They look more like shock absorbers than DC motors. And those ungainly batteries have been greatly decreased in size so that they can be hung on the crossbar of a bicycle. They're narrow enough to keep you from knocking your knees against them when you're working the pedals, but they're also so small now that the practical range of the Electric Go-Pak is less than ten miles.

A ten-mile range is plenty for some people. A large but

still limited number of people would love to glide a few miles to work or to school on an entirely silent mo-ped complete with a derailleur and ten gears for pedaling. Get there, plug it into a battery charger, and eight hours later head home with a fully recharged battery. Great for recreation, too, especially in areas where the climate is too hot for steady pedaling. All in all, the Electric Go-Pak is a clever little machine, but it still has the problems of limited range, limited speed, high cost.

First you have to buy your bicycle, then the Go-Pak—the motors, fittings, batteries, charger. And don't think for a moment that those batteries are going to keep you gliding along forever. As with a car's batteries, they'll wear out. In fact, they'll wear out quicker than an equivalent car's batteries, because it isn't good for a battery to be repeatedly run down to exhaustion and recharged.

The ideal thing for any electric vehicle, mo-ped or otherwise, is a tiny battery that holds hundreds of ampere hours of electricity and doesn't cost a fortune. However, there is no such thing, not even in space vehicles. There are silver batteries and cadmium batteries and power-producing hydrogen cells, all of which are smaller and have higher power densities than the traditional lead sulfate battery. But for a long time to come the average person just won't be able to afford those more exotic forms of portable electricity. And it's the same thing with solar cells.

The best place for the electric vehicle is inside an industrial plant. There they can operate without noise, or atmospheric pollution, and with an electric outlet always close at hand. One successful public transportation applica-

The Solo Electric comes with a battery charger. Though it doesn't yet measure up to the gasoline-powered mo-ped, it does the job for short hauls.

tion of the electric vehicle operates in a similar environment in Denmark.

They call it the Wittkar. It's a tall, short, boxy little four-wheeled vehicle that operates in the downtown streets of Copenhagen. You can't buy the expensive, two-passenger machine and its batteries, but you can rent one by joining the Wittkar organization. You're issued a plastic card that serves as an ignition key for the Wittkar and tells the organization through a computer how long you've used it.

There are Wittkar stations scattered around Copenhagen where you can walk in, insert your card, and drive silently off in a machine whose batteries are fully charged. You drive it close to your downtown destination and leave it at another Wittkar station where it is plugged into a charger to await its next driver. You're billed at the end of the month for the number of hours or kilometers you've driven a Wittkar. This system might be the solution for transportation in the future, when we have nuclear power plants to generate electricity. But of course the system requires an extensive and expensive network of battery recharging stations, the rental and billing system, and the vehicles themselves.

And there are the two- and three-wheeled electric motorcycles produced by Auranthetic Corporation and the two-wheeler made by Daihatsu of Japan, plus others. These are all idealistic, futuristic modes of transportation. Today, however, the gasoline-powered mo-ped exists as the real economy vehicle.

9 You and Your Mo-Ped

Each mo-ped has its own distinctive features, such as speed, carrying capacity, styling, ease of maintenance. There is a mo-ped to fit your particular need, to fit your particular personality. But all mo-peds have certain things in common when it comes to keeping them running in top shape. These are things you can easily do for yourself:

1. Take care of that spark plug. Keep in mind that it is your only source of fire. Keep it clean. Don't let accumulated carbon and lead deposits close the tight space around the electrodes. Keep it properly gapped. As the gap naturally widens with use, close it down to the proper setting before your mo-ped becomes hard to start. Keep an extra plug in your tool kit so you can change plugs on the road without too much delay. Make sure your spark plug is in the correct heat range. All spark plugs may look the same but they are numbered differently, and too cold a plug will make your mo-ped run poorly, while too hot a plug will burn a hole in your piston. You should inspect and clean your

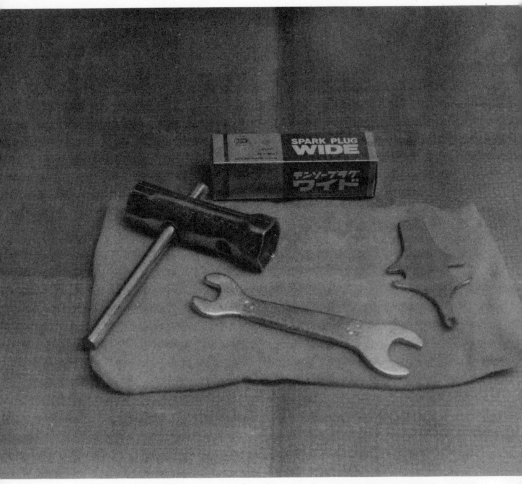

The tool kit that comes with your mo-ped won't be enough for major work, but it will help out in a road emergency. A spare spark plug, the heart of your mo-ped, is a good idea.

spark plug at least once every four hundred miles. And if you can't use the spark plug wrench that comes with the mo-ped, you shouldn't own a mo-ped.

2. Keep your air filter clean. Mo-pedding with a dirty air filter is like trying to run the mile while chewing on a hamburger. Don't be tempted to punch holes in your air cleaner or to remove it completely in hopes of getting souped up performance from your mo-ped. That little air filter also acts to regulate the amount of air your engine needs for peak performance. And of course, it keeps dust and dirt from destroying your bearings and piston rings. And always, after you've cleaned your air filter, make certain that it is properly put back together, with no air leaks.

3. Use the correct amount of oil in your gasoline. If you come across a secondhand mo-ped and don't know what oil mix is recommended, find out before you run it. Check with the dealer for that particular machine or write to the manufacturer, but don't just guess. Too much oil will foul your spark plug and too little will weld your piston and cylinder together. Mix the right amount of oil thoroughly with your gasoline. The best way is to do it in a proper gasoline can. Next best is to add it to your gas tank and then add the gasoline on top of it. Short of adding no oil at all, the worst procedure is to fill up with gasoline and then dump oil in on top of it. The two are completely soluble, but they can stratify if not mixed, with the oil lying on top and the raw gasoline going through your carburetor. Have a care, too, if you loan your mo-ped to anyone. Make sure the borrower understands that the gasoline needs oil.

Here is a nice new piston, ready to carry you thousands of miles on the proper gas/oil mixture.

And use the correct oil. If possible, stick to the oil that's recommended in your owner's manual. Use good two-stroke oil, specifically made to lubricate your kind of engine.

4. When you set out to work on your mo-ped, do so thoughtfully and carefully. Work on it in a clean place, like a garage with a work bench. Get some metric tools. Those in your mo-ped's tool kit are adequate for road repairs, but they are lacking in both number and quality for any more ambitious work. Keep a container such as a coffee can handy to hold the nuts and bolts and washers you remove, and work with your owner's manual just as handy for step by step reference. Just because your mo-ped is a simple, friendly little machine, don't think you can tear into it with a pair of pliers and a crescent wrench out on the front lawn.

5. Keep your spokes tight and your wheels aligned. A spoke tightener from a bicycle or a motorcycle shop will help you do the job in a few minutes every month.

6. Although it's a kick to watch people's reaction to your pedaling backward while the motor is running, don't do it. The pedal on the right is screwed in with right-hand threads, that on the left with left-hand threads. As you pedal normally, the pedals get tighter in the pedal cranks. But when you pedal backward you slowly but surely unscrew the pedals from their sockets.

7. If you have a mo-ped with a battery, see that it is kept properly topped off with distilled water. When the liquid level drops, the battery's plates warp to a point where they touch each other, totally destroying the battery's usefulness. See that your battery is fully charged, even if this means investing four or five dollars in a trickle charger. An

automobile battery charger is just too vigorous for a mo-ped's battery and can burn it up in short order. Because of frequently changing laws laid down by the federal Department of Transportation, your mo-ped might have a battery and might not. It might have turn signals and it might not. It might have a very simple wiring system and its sleek little frame might conceal a whole maze of multicolored wires, all imposed upon the machine by a government that didn't yet understand what a mo-ped was all about. At first glance the Department of Transportation took the mo-ped for a small motorcycle and insisted that all motorcycle lighting laws were applicable to the mo-ped. In the course of taking a second look and backing off on these laws, many mo-peds were made with much more lighting and wiring than is really necessary. Some people like the extra lighting, the oversized head and tail lights and the turn signals, and some people don't. Now these extras are optional in a new mo-ped. But whatever lighting system you have on your mo-ped, take care of it. Watch for a wire that might be rubbed by a wheel or that might be cut by a part of the frame. Know where your fuse is, and carry an extra one with you. If you're doing work on your mo-ped that requires the disconnection of some terminals, make a diagram on a piece of paper to refer to when you're putting it back together. If your mo-ped comes with a schematic wiring diagram, and it should, hang onto it. Keep it at home, in a safe, dry place. You might never use it, but on the other hand it might be very necessary someday. For instance:

On an older machine, especially one without a battery, the lights may gradually grow dim. Its sight is not failing

Oversized headlights are one of the burdens placed on the American version of the world's most economical motor vehicle.

with age as this happens. The problem lies in corrosion. Metallic oxides are slowly building up in the electrical terminals, increasing electrical resistance between them and blocking the flow of current to your lights. To correct it, take the terminals apart, one by one, and clean them. During this operation, that wiring diagram will tell you where each terminal is, so that you don't miss one.

8. Keep your chain or your chains cleaned and oiled and *properly adjusted.* A too tight chain puts a wearing strain on bearings. A chain that is too loose does more than merely rattle around. It snaps and jerks at the rear hub, misaligning gears, and it goes on to snap and jerk at the motor, damaging bearing surfaces and upsetting the ignition timing. A tight chain can easily break, while a loose one gets quickly looser. Before you buy your mo-ped, have a good look at exactly what needs to be done to adjust the chain, and be sure you can do it yourself. Belts are not nearly so critical in their adjustment because they have more give to them than chains, but still they should be adjusted periodically.

9. Ride your mo-ped safely, sensibly. It's a fun machine, safer than a bicycle, but you can still crash on it. It can slip right out from under you on a wet or oily street, so keep an eye out for hazardous road surfaces at all times. Before you know it, this vigilance becomes habit, and you don't need to think about avoiding that slick spot just ahead of you. Be especially careful about braking on questionable road surfaces. Use the rear brake first, and moments later come on with the front brake, even though the front brake has considerably more stopping power than the rear. When the brakes are applied, weight distribution heads for the front

wheel, taking weight off the back tire and robbing it of some of its stopping power. By hitting the rear brake first, you get all of that stopping power you can before the weight distribution heads for the front tire.

Be sure that your reflectors are all in place and that your lights are all functioning. Wear light-colored clothing after dark. Be visible, day or night. Don't rely on a bright-colored machine to increase your visibility to the motorist because the majority of motorists will not see your mo-ped at all. What they will see is you. The human eye is highly conditioned to pick out a human silhouette from the surroundings. Once past you, the average motorist wouldn't be able to say if you were riding on a Solex or a Harley Davidson, but he was probably aware that he passed someone in a white jacket on a two-wheeler. That is the average motorist, and you've got to do what you can to make him know you are sharing the road with him. To be safe, assume that you are completely invisible to the average automobile driver, *and watch out for him.*

That's for the average motorist, the one that scarcely sees you. There is another kind of motorist who is even more dangerous, and this is the kind who very definitely does see you. There are two of this kind. One sees you and recognizes that you have a unique two-wheeler. He is fascinated by it, so much so that he slows down on passing you, swivels around to look at it over his shoulder, and sends his car swerving into your path. He can be a very real hazard to you in his fascination for your clever little machine. He can also be a hazard to your friend who is riding on his mo-ped just ahead of you and who doesn't suspect the rear-ending he's going to get. Watch out for this motorist, too. Look for his head to turn and his hands to turn on the wheel, *and watch out for him.*

The most dangerous motorist of all, though, is the one who very clearly sees you at an intersection, sizes you up, and issues an immediate challenge to you. You can see right through the aggressive look in his eyes and just about read his mind. He—or she—is thinking: *There's another of those darned cyclists, having a good time, carefree, independent. Me and my eight-cylinder gas hog are paying for this road and this stop signal while that cyclist is enjoying it. But wait. That's not a motorcycle, it's just a dinky motorbike! It probably doesn't even run on gas, and it sure couldn't hurt us if it smashed into a fender. We're bumping this stop signal and going through. We can either beat that thing through or it can get the heck out of our way!*

This is a terrible attitude. It does not at all speak well for the sensible, responsible nature of mankind. But it occurs, time and again, and you will certainly see it as you ride the streets on your mo-ped. There is something about the automobile that can change the sweetest, kindliest person into a selfish, aggressive maniac. Expect to meet this maniac at each and every intersection, *and watch out for him most of all.*

10. Have a good time on your mo-ped. That is the most cardinal rule of all. Yes, there are madmen and seemingly blind people sharing the road with you, but learn to smile at

One thing is certain—you'll ride your mo-ped a whole lot more than you'll work on it.

112

them rather than letting them provoke you. It's good for your patience, and it just might help in educating them. Yes, your mo-ped will break down at some point in its life, because it is a mechanical creation, but whatever it is that is wrong with it can certainly be fixed. It is good for your sense of self-esteem when you fix it, and just as good for that self-esteem when you make the decision to get some help with it.

But repairs and road hazards do not appear all that frequently. The primary purpose of your mo-ped is your transportation, your independence, your enjoyment. Know the rules of the road, know the inner workings of your mo-ped, and you will enjoy your mo-ped even more.

Index

INDEX

117

The Author

Jerry Murray is a cycle and automotive specialist who lives and works in San Diego, California. This is his first published book.